The Most Deserving

Catherine Trieschmann

A Samuel French Acting Edition

SAMUELFRENCH.COM
SAMUELFRENCH-LONDON.CO.UK

Copyright © 2014 by Catherine Trieschmann
All Rights Reserved

THE MOST DESERVING is fully protected under the copyright laws of the United States of America, the British Commonwealth, including Canada, and all other countries of the Copyright Union. All rights, including professional and amateur stage productions, recitation, lecturing, public reading, motion picture, radio broadcasting, television and the rights of translation into foreign languages are strictly reserved.

ISBN 978-0-573-70327-0

www.SamuelFrench.com
www.SamuelFrench-London.co.uk

For Production Enquiries

United States and Canada
Info@SamuelFrench.com
1-866-598-8449

United Kingdom and Europe
Plays@SamuelFrench-London.co.uk
020-7255-4302

Each title is subject to availability from Samuel French, depending upon country of performance. Please be aware that *THE MOST DESERVING* may not be licensed by Samuel French in your territory. Professional and amateur producers should contact the nearest Samuel French office or licensing partner to verify availability.

CAUTION: Professional and amateur producers are hereby warned that *THE MOST DESERVING* is subject to a licensing fee. Publication of this play(s) does not imply availability for performance. Both amateurs and professionals considering a production are strongly advised to apply to Samuel French before starting rehearsals, advertising, or booking a theatre. A licensing fee must be paid whether the title(s) is presented for charity or gain and whether or not admission is charged. Professional/Stock licensing fees are quoted upon application to Samuel French.

No one shall make any changes in this title(s) for the purpose of production. No part of this book may be reproduced, stored in a retrieval system, or transmitted in any form, by any means, now known or yet to be invented, including mechanical, electronic, photocopying, recording, videotaping, or otherwise, without the prior written permission of the publisher. No one shall upload this title(s), or part of this title(s), to any social media websites.

For all enquiries regarding motion picture, television, and other media rights, please contact Samuel French.

MUSIC USE NOTE

Licensees are solely responsible for obtaining formal written permission from copyright owners to use copyrighted music in the performance of this play and are strongly cautioned to do so. If no such permission is obtained by the licensee, then the licensee must use only original music that the licensee owns and controls. Licensees are solely responsible and liable for all music clearances and shall indemnify the copyright owners of the play(s) and their licensing agent, Samuel French, against any costs, expenses, losses and liabilities arising from the use of music by licensees. Please contact the appropriate music licensing authority in your territory for the rights to any incidental music.

IMPORTANT BILLING AND CREDIT REQUIREMENTS

If you have obtained performance rights to this title, please refer to your licensing agreement for important billing and credit requirements.

THE MOST DESERVING was originally developed and produced by the Denver Center Theatre Company (Kent Thompson, Artistic Director) in Denver, Colorado on October 11, 2013. The performance was directed by Shelley Butler, with sets by David Barber, costumes by Leah Pichl, lighting by Jane Spencer, sound by Tyler Nelson, and dramaturgy by Abigail Gonda. The Production Stage Manager was Rachel Ducat. The cast was as follows:

JOLENE ATKINSON	Judith Hawking
TED ATKINSON	Sam Gregory
LIZ CHANG	Rebecca Hirota
EDIE KELCH	Jeanne Paulsen
DWAYNE DEAN	Craig Bockhorn
EVERETT WHITESIDE	Jonathan Earl Peck

THE MOST DESERVING was subsequently produced by the Women's Project Theater (Julie Crosby, Producing Artistic Director) at the New York City Center in New York City on March 30, 2014. The performance was directed by Shelley Butler, with sets by David Barber, costumes by Donald Sanders, lighting by Traci Klainer Polimeni, sound by Leon Rothenberg, and dramaturgy by Abigail Gonda. The Production Stage Manager was Jess Johnston. The cast was as follows:

JOLENE ATKINSON	Veanne Cox
TED ATKINSON	Daniel Pearce
LIZ CHANG	Jennifer Lim
EDIE KELCH	Kristin Griffith
DWAYNE DEAN	Adam Lefevre
EVERETT WHITESIDE	Ray Anthony Thomas

CHARACTERS

JOLENE ATKINSON – late 40s–50s. Head of the Ellis County Arts Council. Fit, smart, energetic and controlling. A native Kansan. Caucasian.

TED ATKINSON – early 50s. Jolene's husband. Originally from a suburb of Manchester, England. A bit of a burn out. Reporter at the local paper.

LIZ CHANG – 30s. An assistant art professor at the local community college. Intelligent but her ambition outstrips her ability. Asian-American.

EDIE KELCH – 60s–70s. A recent widow in the midst of an identity crisis. A native Kansan. Caucasian.

DWAYNE DEAN – 50s–60s. Recently laid off from the automobile industry. An artist. A native Kansan. Caucasian.

EVERETT WHITESIDE – 40s–60s. A paraplegic, self-taught artist. A native Kansan. African American.

SETTING

Ellis County, Kansas: an art gallery, Ted and Jolene's bedroom, Edie's living room, and Everett's barn studio

TIME

The Present

AUTHOR'S NOTES

"/" indicates an interruption
"*" indicates continuity when dialogue follows dialogue earlier than the line immediately preceding it

Production Note: No artwork discussed should be seen by the audience, leaving its merits or lack thereof to the imagination.

Special thanks to Peter Ellenstein for his early encouragement of the work and to Kent Thompson for directing the first reading then agreeing to produce it one year later. I worked with three amazing dramaturgs on this play: mad genius Tom Bryant, inspiration personified Liz Engleman, and the ultimate connoisseur Abigail Gonda. The brilliant and intrepid Shelley Butler directed the play in Denver and New York and the play is far, far better for it. Thanks to my agent Derek Zasky for walking beside me, even when I don't make him much money. Thanks to Hedgebrook for the best three weeks of my life, during which I was able to revise the play, and to Julie Crosby for her commitment not only to this play but to my body of work. And finally, to my husband Carl and my two girls, Sophie and Martha, thank you for giving me the time and space to write and so much more.

For my father, Jim Trieschmann, who begged me not to go into the arts, then gave me his full and unabashed support when I did.

Scene One

(A small, provincial art gallery in Ellis County, Kansas.)

(EDIE, TED, DWAYNE, LIZ and JOLENE sit in a semi-circle of folding chairs. They all have packets of papers in front of them. JOLENE meticulously reads the budget aloud. DWAYNE tries to keep his eyes open. TED surreptitiously messes with his phone. EDIE has placed her mind elsewhere. LIZ looks like she wants to kill herself or someone else.)

JOLENE. Five hundred and twenty-three dollars and forty-two cents.

Posters.

Three hundred and sixty-seven dollars and sixty-nine cents.

Programs.

Three hundred and sixty-eight dollars and seventy-two cents.

Postcards.

Two hundred and eighty-six dollars and ninety-three cents.

Postage.

One hundred and thirty-three dollars and six cents.

Hardware.

Six hundred and seventy four dollars and twenty-six cents.

Framing.

Two thousand and four hundred –

LIZ. I don't mean to interrupt but –

JOLENE. Yes?

LIZ. Is this really necessary?

(Everyone looks up at **LIZ**, *startled.)*

JOLENE. You're new.

LIZ. I am.

JOLENE. Two thousand and four hundred and fifty dollars.
Prize money.
Five hundred and forty-seven dollars and ninety-eight cents.
Transportation.
Three hundred and sixty dollars and two cents.
Accommodations.
And lastly,
Five hundred dollars.
Guest Artist Stipend.

DWAYNE. And that's five hundred we can save next year.

JOLENE.	**EDIE.**
Here, here.	Oh yes.

(They all laugh, except **LIZ**.*)*

LIZ. What – did he do something? I thought his workshop was top notch.

TED. Yeah, it was.

JOLENE. Nothing special, mind you.

LIZ. My students adored him. They came back all flush and inspired.

DWAYNE. Maybe he was more effective with the younger crowd.

LIZ. Isn't that what we want?

TED. Yes.

JOLENE. The workshop wasn't the problem. The problem was with the adjudication.

EDIE. Oh my.

LIZ. I don't understand.

JOLENE. Were you there?

LIZ. Yes.

JOLENE. Did you see the painting he gave the blue ribbon to?

LIZ. Yes. I thought the brushwork was energetic and the colors vibrant. I wasn't surprised it won.

EDIE. Oh dear.

DWAYNE. I think it's fair to say, taste is more liberal at the college.

EDIE. Some of our supporters were offended.

LIZ. Why? Because the girl was nude? Would our supporters be offended by Michelangelo? By Leonardo Da Vinci?

JOLENE. Of course not.

TED. *(overlapping)*
Yes.

JOLENE. What? No, they wouldn't, Ted. I think I know. I'm the one who fields the complaints. And what are you doing? Are you texting?

TED. No.

JOLENE. I can see your phone. Who are you texting?

TED. I'm not texting. I'm playing scrabble.

JOLENE. Put it away, Ted, for crying out loud. The problem was not that the girl was nude. The problem was it turned out to be Heather Dinkle.

EDIE. Poor Pam.

LIZ. Pam?

EDIE. Pam Dinkle, Heather's mother. She's married to Bobby Dinkle, Dinkle's Dry Cleaning?

LIZ. So the mother was embarrassed. That's understandable, but there's no shame in modeling nude for a piece of art.

JOLENE. Heather Dinkle is fourteen.

LIZ. Oh.

JOLENE. Next order of business. Ted, do I need to confiscate your phone?

TED. Does she have that kind of power?

DWAYNE. Yes.

JOLENE. Dwayne, why don't you bring us up to date on the Living Wage Grant.

DWAYNE. Alrighty. Thanks to Edie and her late husband Vernon –

EDIE. God rest his soul.

DWAYNE. Yes. As I was saying, thanks to Edie and Vernon –

EDIE. May he rest in peace.

DWAYNE. Amen.

JOLENE. We've received a matching grant from the Living Wage Foundation to support a visual artist here in Ellis County. The award is twenty thousand dollars and a show at the gallery.

LIZ. That's terrific.

DWAYNE. We have a few candidates to consider. The guidelines provided by the Foundation are pretty narrow.

LIZ. What are they?

DWAYNE. I have them here somewhere –

JOLENE. The artist must have lived in Ellis County for five years. He must demonstrate both artistic excellence and financial need and should preferably be an underrepresented American voice.

LIZ. Oh my God – I know the perfect person!

JOLENE. The deadline has passed.

LIZ. We can extend it, can't we? I mean, we are the Council.

TED. I don't see why not.

JOLENE. Because that would be unfair to the candidates who worked hard to get their applications in on time.

DWAYNE. It's important that everyone has the same chance.

LIZ. How does extending the deadline make the process unfair? If anything, it broadens our scope. Are you familiar with Everett Whiteside?

JOLENE. Never heard of him.

EDIE. Is he related to Betsey Whiteside?

LIZ. Not that I know of.

DWAYNE. *(overlapping)*
Didn't Betsey have a brother who was lobotomized?

EDIE. Yes – is that who you're talking about?

LIZ. Everett lives just outside town. He's confined to a wheelchair and living on disability. He'd be the perfect recipient. He's African American –

EDIE. Then he's definitely not Betsey's brother. Betsey's people were Norwegian.

LIZ. And most importantly, he's a genius.

JOLENE. So what does this genius do?

LIZ. He creates these extraordinary sculptures depicting religious subjects out of trash.

TED. Huh.

LIZ. No, I'm telling you, it's profound.

TED. Are you talking about the Trash Man?

LIZ. I've never heard –

TED. Yeah, the Trash Man! He lives off old forty, and his barn is covered in all this crazy shit he makes out of trash.

LIZ. Yes, the barn, that's where he works, but I wouldn't call it crazy shit.

TED. That came out wrong.

DWAYNE. I'm not an expert, but if it looks like it came from the dump, then it ain't art.

LIZ. It's unconventional, I know, but Everett is part of this movement of outsider artists…that is, artists who haven't been formally trained…

JOLENE. We know what outsider art is.

LIZ. Well, I don't like the term, I think it "others" the artists.

JOLENE. Then why did you use it?

LIZ. The point is, the Visionary Art Museum in Kansas City is interested in Everett upon my recommendation.

JOLENE. Are you his agent?

LIZ. No, I'm a fan.

JOLENE. Well, this is all very interesting, but we aren't going to give the largest single grant this organization has ever awarded to the Trash Man without going through a proper application process.

LIZ. But he fits all the criteria to a T!

DWAYNE. I just don't think we should be giving away twenty-thousand dollars to an "outsider" artist, when there are so many deserving artists living inside town.

LIZ. Like who?

DWAYNE. I have the applications right here: Erin Hernandez.

JOLENE. Now her quilts are lovely.

TED. Is she a minority?

DWAYNE. She's a Hernandez.

JOLENE. By marriage.

TED. Does that count?

LIZ. It shouldn't.

TED. I agree with Liz.

EDIE. It's irrelevant. She doesn't have financial need.

DWAYNE. But she's always going on about how hard it is to make a living as an artist.

EDIE. It's all a show. Her father owns half the mineral rights in Ellis County.

JOLENE. That's right. He does.

DWAYNE. Who knew? So long Erin Hernandez.

JOLENE. Who else?

DWAYNE. Rick Duffy. His need is undeniable. He's a high school teacher.

JOLENE. I just love his Iris series.

EDIE. Oh, me too. It reminds me of Van Gogh.

JOLENE. That's so insightful, Edie.

LIZ. If Van Gogh had been derivative and mediocre.

JOLENE. Now Edie has a great eye. Perhaps Rick's work is just too subtle for your taste.

LIZ. Look, Rick Duffy is a nice man and a fine artist, but a white, male oil painter does not a minority voice make.

JOLENE. Rick is Native American, part Native American.

LIZ. Which part, his spleen?

JOLENE. His grandmother was a member of the Sioux tribe.

EDIE. Great-grandmother.

JOLENE. That makes him what...one quarter.

TED. One-eighth.

EDIE. Or maybe she was half-Sioux.

TED. One-sixteenth.

DWAYNE. Either way, my ancestors would have shot his great-grandmother without pause.

JOLENE. The point is: he's a minority. Is that it?

DWAYNE. Well, I know this is a little unorthodox, but I'd like to throw my own hat into the proverbial ring. As you all know, after thirty-five years of service in the automobile industry, I got laid off last year, so the financial need is there. Trust me, it is there.

LIZ. Are you one-sixteenth Sioux too?

DWAYNE. No, no. I can't make that claim, but the grant says "preferably" an underrepresented American voice. It doesn't say it has to be. Now I know I'm new to the game of art, but I think we can all agree I've taken to it like a fish to water. I tell you what, I'd like nothing more than to take a year to finish my Vice-Presidential series. Think about it. You see portraits of the Presidents everywhere, art museums, everywhere, but not Vice-Presidents. There's a gap. I think it'd be a solid contribution to the field.

LIZ. What field?

DWAYNE. The field of art. I'd recuse myself from the selection process of course.

(Silence. Everyone is horrified.)

JOLENE. Dwayne, I just want to congratulate you for being so brave. Putting yourself out there like this, that's just super.

EDIE. Extremely brave.

DWAYNE. Thank you, ladies.

JOLENE. Why don't we do this? Since the grant says "preferably" an under-represented voice, let's table your application for the time being, until we fully consider the minority candidates, like Rick Duffy.

LIZ. Good idea!

EDIE. *(overlapping)*
Great!

TED. *(overlapping)*
Yeah.

DWAYNE. *(disappointed)*
Alright. If you think that's best. I'll concede to the majority.

LIZ. And in the spirit of giving our minority artists full consideration, I propose we all visit Everett and view his work together.

EDIE. May I ask you something, dear?

LIZ. Of course.

EDIE. You said his work was of a religious nature?

LIZ. Yes.

EDIE. But it's made out of trash.

LIZ. That's right.

EDIE. I don't have a problem with that, I'm very open-minded, I'm a Methodist, but might it strike the Catholics in the community as sacrilegious?

LIZ. Maybe but isn't great art supposed to provoke?

JOLENE. Not in Kansas.

LIZ. What's astonishing about Everett's work, Edie, is that he finds trash and transforms it. For example, he constructed this twenty-foot angel out of smashed dog food cans. She hangs from the back wall of the barn, and when you open the door, the sun shines directly on her. I'm not a religious person, but the sight of that angel, well, she unmoored me.

EDIE. Vernon is with the angels now.

LIZ. You must see it. You must all see it.

JOLENE. Let's put it to a vote. All in favor of throwing a fair and objective application process to the wind in order to consider the Trash Man, raise your hand.

(**LIZ** *raises her hand immediately.*)

(**EDIE** *raises her hand.*)

Is that it then?

TED. No.

(**TED** *raises his hand.*)

(**LIZ** *is surprised and pleased.*)

(**JOLENE** *is not.*)

Right. Meeting adjourned. Who else wants coffee?

(**TED** *quickly escapes.* **DWAYNE** *and* **EDIE** *are close on his heels.*)

EDIE. Decaf.

DWAYNE. *(overlapping)*
Count me in.

(**JOLENE** *eyes* **LIZ**, *as she gathers her things.*)

JOLENE. Bob said you were a firecracker.

LIZ. Bob?

JOLENE. Chairman of the City Council Bob Duffy?

LIZ. Oh right. I sat beside him at the Senior Banquet.

JOLENE. That's why he recommended you?

LIZ. I did share some of my ideas for raising art awareness in our community. There's just so much potential here!

JOLENE. Such as?

LIZ. Oh you know, the usual: enrichment classes, library lectures, a National Center for Visionary Art, curated by Professor Liz Chang.

JOLENE. Let me ask you something, Liz. Do you know how hard it is to raise money for the arts in Western Kansas?

LIZ. I think I have some idea.

JOLENE. It's like trying to squeeze water from a sponge in the middle of the Serengeti.

LIZ. Okay.

JOLENE. It's taken me over a decade to get this organization up and running, including but not limited to acquiring a permanent space, attracting viable donors, and lobbying the City Council relentlessly, until they made my position full-time, since I was, after all, working sixty hours a week anyway.

LIZ. Thanks for laying all the groundwork!

JOLENE. The Board is a rubber stamp to all my hard work. Don't tread on me.

Scene Two

(**TED** *and* **JOLENE***'s Bedroom.*)

(**TED** *turns on some music, something from the Seventies, maybe The Grateful Dead. He gets his groove on, while he pours himself some peppermint schnapps. He's wearing a thoroughly worn out undershirt with yellow stains around the armpits, tidy whiteys or boxers and black knee socks.*)

(**JOLENE** *enters, wearing an old house gown.* **TED** *flops on the bed and hides behind his football (British) magazine.*)

(**JOLENE** *turns off the music.*)

(*She turns on some soft jazz. He doesn't protest. She gets in bed beside him.*)

(*pause*)

TED. Get on with it then.

JOLENE. What?

TED. If you're going to have my head, I'd just as soon get it over with.

JOLENE. I'm not in the mood.

TED. Since when?

JOLENE. It's gotten a bit old, don't cha think?

TED. Yeah.

JOLENE. Good.

TED. *(perking up)*
   Cool.

JOLENE. Anything interesting at the paper today?

TED. I didn't go in.

JOLENE. Why not?

TED. No news today.

JOLENE. Nothing?

TED. Well, Burt Hoffenwenter died.

JOLENE. Isn't obituaries one of your beats?

TED. Twenty-five bucks a story does not make a beat. It makes coffee. Maybe a haircut.

JOLENE. You're right. Why bother? *(pause)* You know what?

TED. What?

JOLENE. I have an idea. Why don't you quit the paper?

TED. Really?

JOLENE. Yes, take a year off to really find yourself. You deserve it.

TED. You're joking.

JOLENE. No. Now that Joey's out of the house, why not? Take a year off. Search your soul. What do you really want to do? You used to want to be a rock journalist, remember?

TED. Yeah, imagine sitting down with Jerry Garcia and having a real heart to heart. I could still do that, you know. It's not too late.

JOLENE. Well, it is for Jerry.

TED. Yeah, not Jerry, of course. But Bobby. Is he alive?

JOLENE. I don't know, but you could do some research.

TED. *(uncertain)*
Like, at the library?

JOLENE. Or the internet.

TED. Yeah, I could do that. Good idea. Thanks.

JOLENE. You're welcome. *(pause)* It's stuffy in here. Are you warm?

TED. I'm comfortable.

JOLENE. Must be the humidity.

TED. What humidity? We live on the high plains.

JOLENE. I'm about to suffocate.

(She unbuttons her housecoat to reveal a sexy, lingerie number underneath. Stockings, snaps, corset, bustier, etc...)

*(**TED** bursts out laughing.)*

TED. What's this then?

JOLENE. Nothing for your information. I just wanted to feel feminine for a change. For myself. It's not for you.

TED. I wouldn't dream of it. It's not my taste.

(JOLENE opens her magazine and pretends to read, clearly hurt.)

(TED returns to his schnapps and his football.)

JOLENE. What do you mean, it's not your taste?

TED. I prefer fewer bells and whistles on a woman is all.

JOLENE. I make an effort in the bedroom for once, and you say, "Jolly ho – it's not my taste."

TED. You said it was for you.

JOLENE. I said that to cover, you jack-ass.

TED. How was I supposed to know that?

JOLENE. What kind of imbecile thinks his wife puts on a garter belt for herself?

TED. You took me by surprise. You look very nice all tarted up.

JOLENE. Do you find me attractive at all?

TED. You're very fit for a woman your age.

JOLENE. Why do you bother staying in this marriage?

TED. For the sake of the children, of course. Kidding! I'm only kidding!

(JOLENE smacks him with her magazine repeatedly and with real vigor.)

Oh, come here, my little fruit tart. Let me get a good look at you. Yeah, I get it. You've got this here. Lovely. *(He gives her thigh high a little snap.)* And that there. Just scrumptious. Now what does this do? I see. How inventive. And that. It pushes those up higher than they've been in a long while. Fantastic. All in all, I'd say you're a perfect peach tart.

JOLENE. Oh, for God's sake, please stop talking.

(She kisses him long and hard, and it's kind of nice for a change.)

(What a fucking surprise for them both.)

(They sit back, a little stunned.)

TED. I'll just get a re-fill then. Want one?

JOLENE. Yes.

*(**TED** pours two glasses of peppermint schnapps, while **JOLENE** arranges herself on the pillows.)*

TED. Here you go.

*(**JOLENE** takes a drink and tries to hide how awful it is.)*

*(**TED** downs his.)*

Alright then!

(He carefully lies down next to her. He's nervous. They sit there for a beat. He fiddles with her stocking snap. It won't give.)

Your stocking seems impervious to my charms.

*(**JOLENE** sets down her drink.)*

JOLENE. Never mind that.

(She takes charge. She sits up and authoritatively rolls him over on his stomach. She sits on his buttocks and begins to massage his back.)

TED. Oh God. Oh God. This is heaven. I'm sorry I laughed at you. I'm a cold, lazy bastard who deserves to be shot. I promise to wash up more. I promise. Oh God. That is the spot. Oh. My. Bliss.

(She massages him for awhile, then slows.)

JOLENE. You know, I've been wondering something all day.

TED. What?

JOLENE. You do know who Rick Duffy's father is, right?

TED. Hmmmmm?

JOLENE. Rick's father is Bob Duffy, Chairman of the City Council.

TED. Mmmmmm…what of it?

JOLENE. Our budget goes up for approval in two weeks. Now Bob Duffy is a very discrete man, but there have been hints.

TED. Hmmmm…Lower. Harder. Lower.

(She complies.)

JOLENE. I am under the impression that if Rick were to receive the Living Wage Grant, then our budget request would go unchallenged.

TED. Mmmmmmmm.

JOLENE. And since Vernon's no longer on the City Council, we really need Bob Duffy's support.

TED. Uhhhhhhhhhh.

JOLENE. So you see, that changes everything, and now that you have the full context, you can change your vote.

*(**TED** sits up abruptly.)*

TED. Is that what all this is about?

JOLENE. What?

TED. This seduction!

JOLENE. Don't be ridiculous.

TED. It is, isn't it?

JOLENE. If all I needed was an extra vote, I could get that with Edie in three minutes.

TED. Admit it.

JOLENE. You've had one too many, I think.

TED. Admit it.

JOLENE. It's made you paranoid.

TED. Why won't you just admit it?

JOLENE. You always get paranoid when you drink peppermint schnapps. I don't know why I allow it in the house.

TED. Admit it!

JOLENE. Fine, I admit it! Of course, I was just trying to get your vote. Why else would I want to have sex with someone who has piss on his undershirt?

TED. It's not piss; it's perspiration.
JOLENE. In that case, take me now big boy.
TED. What about my year off?
JOLENE. A year off from what?

>   (**JOLENE** *climbs back into bed and opens her magazine.*)

Scene Three

(**EVERETT**'s *Barn*)

(**EVERETT**'s *at his worktable, working on a new piece.* **LIZ** *enters, bringing a couple of oranges as a gift.*)

EVERETT. Sister Liz!

LIZ. Hi Everett.

EVERETT. You want some tea? I just brewed some up.

LIZ. No thanks.

EVERETT. You sure? Got some rice crispy treats too. Loretta brought 'em by. She's still trying to get her some of this. I told her there ain't nothing here for her, but she don't listen. That woman is delusional.

LIZ. Certifiable. Listen, I have good news.

EVERETT. Oh yeah?

LIZ. You know how I'm on that Arts Council?

EVERETT. Uh huh.

LIZ. Well, they're considering you for a grant!

EVERETT. You sure you don't want no tea? Just the right mix of sugar and mint.

LIZ. Did you hear what I said? You're being considered for a grant.

EVERETT. Is it in the bank?

LIZ. No –

EVERETT. Then forgive me, if I don't throw you a parade.

LIZ. It's twenty thousand dollars.

EVERETT. You got my attention.

LIZ. Good. Because I told the council all about your work and how moved I was by the angel. They can't wait to see her.

EVERETT. They want to see the angel?

LIZ. Yes!

EVERETT. Well shit.

LIZ. What's the problem?

EVERETT. That angel has been reunited with her God.

LIZ. What are you talking about?

EVERETT. I took her down. She don't exist no more.

LIZ. Well put her back up.

EVERETT. I can't.

LIZ. Why not?

EVERETT. Cause Loretta took her bits and pieces to the dump.

LIZ. You threw her away?

EVERETT. Yes!

LIZ. But why would you do that? She was your masterpiece!

EVERETT. I got tired of looking at her.

LIZ. Well shit!

EVERETT. That's what I'm saying!

LIZ. I have been busting my ass all over town for you, hell, all over the state. What am I going to tell the Visionary Art Museum in Kansas City? They wanted to acquire that piece!

EVERETT. You can tell those assholes, Everett Whiteside ain't interested in them.

LIZ. What? Last time I was here you were thrilled about the museum. We looked through the catalog, we kicked back some beers.

EVERETT. I looked that place up on the inter-webs, and they don't show nothing but art by crazy people.

LIZ. No, that's not true. They show work by untrained artists –

EVERETT. Half them muthafuckers are sending their shit straight from the asylum.

LIZ. Okay, yes, but not all. Some are like you, self-taught.

EVERETT. I do not belong there, Liz. I am not crazy, and I am not ignorant, and you can quote me on that.

LIZ. Is that why you destroyed the angel, because you didn't want her shown at the museum?

EVERETT. No, I took that bitch down, cause she was looking at me funny.

LIZ. That museum is a big deal, Everett. When they buy something, people follow.

EVERETT. Wait a minute. You said buy. They wanted to buy her?

LIZ. Yes, they were very interested in buying her.

EVERETT. Now you didn't tell me that.

LIZ. I did –

EVERETT. No, you said they wanted to acquire her.

LIZ. I don't remember my exact words –

EVERETT. You said acquire. You did not say buy. I would have remembered if you had said buy.

LIZ. Well, what did you think acquire meant?

EVERETT. I thought it meant they was gonna drive down here in a pick-up truck and stick her in the back.

LIZ. No, they were going to pay you for her.

EVERETT. Well shit. I got bills to pay.

LIZ. I know. That's why I was so hopeful about the museum sale. You could pay your back taxes.

EVERETT. Shit. Shitshitshitshitshitshit –

LIZ. Hey, it's going to be okay.

EVERETT. No, it ain't. Uncle Sam is on my back.

LIZ. I know.

EVERETT. Trying to make me bend over and take it.

LIZ. I understand.

EVERETT. He's in there now.

LIZ. Where?

EVERETT. Inside my asshole, hammering away, bang, bang, bang

LIZ. Hey – can I have some of that tea? All of a sudden I'm parched.

EVERETT. You want some tea?

LIZ. That'd be great.

EVERETT. I got some fresh mint from the garden this morning.

LIZ. Perfect.

(**EVERETT** *wheels over to his little refrigerator and gets her some tea.*)

You know, one could argue that your willingness to destroy your work is evidence of your authenticity as an artist. It's the ultimate resistance to commodification. Art can't be bought or sold if it's destroyed.

EVERETT. What are you talking about?

LIZ. Damage control. You know that book I'm writing? I could do a whole chapter on work you've destroyed. I have pictures of the angel at least. How often do you destroy your work? I mean, was this the first time, or do you dismantle things often?

EVERETT. I don't keep track.

LIZ. Did you destroy anything else this week?

(**EVERETT** *shrugs.*)

Was anyone else looking at you funny, giving you the evil eye?

EVERETT. Sampson.

LIZ. You mean, the bust with all the hair?

(**EVERETT** *nods.*)

What did you do with it?

EVERETT. I got rid of him.

LIZ. How? Did you throw him away? Set him on fire?

EVERETT. I gave that muthafucker a makeover.

LIZ. Can I see?

(**EVERETT** *gestures to the work. It is out of sight, either in a nook of the barn or perhaps in a box.*)

Wow. Is this John the Baptist?

EVERETT. Yep.

LIZ. Why is his head covered in bees?

EVERETT. Cause he eats honey. You like him?

LIZ. Like him? I could just kiss you.

EVERETT. You ain't my type, Liz.

LIZ. Everett, this is just extraordinary. He's dirty and disgusting and holy all at the same time. You're a genius. A flat out genius, you know that?

EVERETT. Yes.

LIZ. This would make a great book cover. Please don't destroy him. At least until I come back with my camera.

EVERETT. You sold your book?

LIZ. No, I have to finish the book before I sell it.

EVERETT. But somebody's gonna buy it?

LIZ. I'm optimistic.

EVERETT. You gonna give me a piece of that?

LIZ. Oh, it's not that kind of book. People don't make money off academic books.

EVERETT. Why they publish them, then?

LIZ. Tenure.

EVERETT. Liz.

LIZ. Yeah.

EVERETT. I need money.

LIZ. I know you do, Everett.

EVERETT. I got Uncle Sam inside my asshole, hammering away, bang, bang, bang! You know what that feels like?

LIZ. Not entirely, no.

EVERETT. Try, Liz, try. Imagine Uncle Sam eating away at your – *(cunt)*

LIZ. Forget the book. Forget the museum. Let's focus on the grant. I've filled out the application, but the council wants to interview you.

EVERETT. Interview me?

LIZ. Yes. So you'll need to clean up. Do you have a suit?

EVERETT. Same suit I got married in. Tried to burn it when Jocelyn left me but that polyester wouldn't catch fire. That suit is invincible.

LIZ. The point is you need to look as professional as possible. And we'll practice interviewing.

EVERETT. Nothing to worry about, Liz. I've aced every interview I've ever had.

LIZ. We'll see. But Everett, the most important thing is, you cannot talk about Uncle Sam.

EVERETT. But he is living in my –

LIZ. I know where he is living, and I know he's been harassing you for a very long time, but the arts council isn't going to understand like I do.

EVERETT. Why? Do they work for him?

LIZ. No, but trust me, they will not understand.

EVERETT. I don't trust nobody who works for Uncle Sam.

LIZ. You don't have to trust anybody but me. Do you think you can do that?

EVERETT. You really think I'm a genius?

LIZ. Absolutely.

EVERETT. Then I trust you.

Scene Four

(JOLENE *stands in* EDIE*'s atrociously decorated chintzy, living room, with a particularly offensive floral couch front and center.*)

(EDIE *enters with a tea trolley.*)

JOLENE. *(pointing to the couch)*
Is this new?

EDIE. I've had it for ages.

JOLENE. That's strange. I could have sworn it was new.

EDIE. No.

JOLENE. How could I have missed it?

EDIE. It used to be in the sunroom.

JOLENE. That must be it.

EDIE. I've been re-arranging the furniture.

JOLENE. Doing a little Feng Shui.

EDIE. I should hope not!

JOLENE. Well, you just have a perfect eye for color.

EDIE. Interior design was always a passion, you know.

JOLENE. No, I didn't.

EDIE. Yes, I would have been an interior designer, if Junior hadn't come along so quickly.

JOLENE. Good thing he did.

EDIE. Excuse me?

JOLENE. You were meant to be a Mother.

EDIE. You know, Junior said the funniest thing yesterday, what was it? Oh yes. He said, "Now that Dad's dead, are you going to keep giving away all our money?"

JOLENE. What a little joker – how is Junior?

EDIE. Fine, considering.

JOLENE. It's so difficult.

EDIE. Yes. It's so hard on all of us. Vernon was such a virile man.

JOLENE. Larger than life.

EDIE. Of course, Junior's also having the worst luck at work. He's selling office supplies at Maxwell's, and do you know they only work on commission?

JOLENE. I didn't know that.

EDIE. This economy is terribly hard on white men.

JOLENE. It's a hard time to be in office supplies, yes.

(They sip their tea.)

You know, Vernon was a very special man. There wouldn't be an Arts Council without him. Not only did he raise money for the gallery year after year; he championed us against the less progressive conservatives on the City Council.

EDIE. Vernon was a very progressive conservative.

JOLENE. So progressive you could almost mistake him for a Democrat.

EDIE. Not that progressive.

JOLENE. No, he was a true American. And a great patron of the arts. In fact, I consider the Arts Council his legacy. Whenever I have a tough decision to make, I always think: what would Vernon do? WWVD. Anyway, Vernon understood what it takes to keep the arts afloat in a rural community.

EDIE. He did.

JOLENE. Number one: money.

EDIE. You don't have to tell me.

JOLENE. Number two: community support. And you know what galvanizes our community more than anything?

EDIE. A liberal President.

JOLENE. Seeing a local boy make good. Rick Duffy grew up here. His ancestors lived off the land before the pilgrims even hit Plymouth rock.

EDIE. Of course, Everett Whiteside is from Ellis County too.

JOLENE. Rick Duffy has dedicated his life to art education. Vernon would have appreciated that.

EDIE. Jolene.

JOLENE. Yes, Edie.

EDIE. Six months ago, you sat in this very room and asked for ten thousand dollars to match the Living Wage Grant, while Vernon sat on this couch, his prostate covered in cancer.

JOLENE. Was it this couch?

EDIE. This very couch.

JOLENE. I thought this couch was in the sunroom.

EDIE. He agreed to match the grant.

JOLENE. Which was very generous.

EDIE. It's what Vernon wanted.

JOLENE. He understood vision.

EDIE. Every extra cent went to either the Arts Council or the NRA.

JOLENE. For which we are truly grateful.

EDIE. I don't expect special treatment.

JOLENE. Of course not.

EDIE. I'm certainly not asking for special treatment.

JOLENE. No.

EDIE. But three months ago, I donated a portrait of Vernon to the gallery.

JOLENE. Yes, I've been meaning –

EDIE. A portrait of a man who donated ten thousand dollars on his deathbed.

JOLENE. For the record, I didn't know he had cancer when I asked.

EDIE. But he did.

JOLENE. Yes.

EDIE. I would like to see that portrait on permanent display.

JOLENE. Edie, I've been meaning to tell you, that painting needs some serious preservation work.

EDIE. Fiddlesticks.

JOLENE. It's a full-length portrait. We need time to make room –

EDIE. Excuses.

JOLENE. I just wonder if the community is ready for that kind of graphic violence.

EDIE. You know, for someone who works in the arts, Jolene, you're really quite a prude.

JOLENE. I'm not thinking of myself. Think about the children who visit the gallery. Vernon is holding a decapitated head.

EDIE. I'm well aware of what's in the painting, Jolene. It hung over our bed for years.

JOLENE. Yes.

EDIE. But now that Vernon's gone, I just can't…it's too painful to stare at his portrait, in the same bed where we made love night after night.

JOLENE. I understand.

EDIE. But I refuse to dishonor his memory by letting it rot in some basement.

JOLENE. Of course. You're right, Edie. You're absolutely right. Vernon's portrait deserves to be on permanent display. Somewhere private.

EDIE. Oh, I know – we can hang it at your house!

JOLENE. My house?

EDIE. Since Vernon meant so much to you.

JOLENE. He did, but I'm not sure it would match –

EDIE. Oh it would match your dining room perfectly!

JOLENE. You think?

EDIE. Didn't you just tell me I had a perfect eye for color?

JOLENE. I would love to display Vernon's portrait, Edie, I would. I just worry about Ted. You know, he was always so intimated by Vernon. I think being reminded of another's man's…prowess day after day might just do him in.

EDIE. Vernon was an Alpha male.

JOLENE. And Ted is not.

EDIE. You have a point.

JOLENE. Oh, I know! Why don't you donate the portrait to the NRA!

EDIE. They do appreciate graphic violence.

JOLENE. I'll make the phone call tomorrow.

EDIE. Thank you.

JOLENE. Now, about the living wage grant –

EDIE. Oh dear, I don't know what's come over me, but Lady Grey did not do the trick. I'm absolutely exhausted.

JOLENE. Really? Me too.

EDIE. Let's call it an afternoon.

JOLENE. I know – why don't I drive you to Mr. Whiteside's studio in the morning, so we can chat before the interview?

EDIE. Fine.

JOLENE. I'll be here bright and early.

EDIE. Yes, dear, you always are.

Scene Five

(EVERETT's Barn. EVERETT, washed up and dressed in a suit, sits for his interview. EDIE, DWAYNE, TED, LIZ and JOLENE are present.)

JOLENE. Thank you for having us to your studio today, Mr. Whiteside.

EVERETT. Happy to have you.

JOLENE. Edie, why don't you get us started?

EDIE. Mr. Whiteside, your work is rather unique. Could you contextualize it for us?

LIZ. *(to EVERETT)*
   Just tell them what inspires you.

JOLENE. Actually, that's not what Edie said.

LIZ. The question was a little vague.

JOLENE. I don't think it was vague at all. Everett, can you contextualize your work for us or not?

   (pause)

LIZ. Everett?

   (He lifts his finger to silence LIZ.)

EVERETT. I work in the tradition of what is called outsider art. That is, artists who have no formal training. While traditionally overlooked by the art world, we are increasingly gaining notice for our originality and unique vision. In fact, there are museums in major metropolitan areas dedicated solely to our kind of work. I am proud to be following in the footsteps of internationally known artists, like Leon Kennedy, Norbot Foote, and Ginny Wright, all celebrated artists without training, like myself.

JOLENE. Why don't you just share with us what inspires you? In your own words.

EVERETT. I draw my inspiration from three things: found objects, the word of God, and my own lived experiences.

DWAYNE. And what drew you to making art out of trash… I mean, found objects?

EVERETT. Oh I've been making shit outta shit for as long as I can remember.

LIZ. Everett, your ability to work long, arduous hours despite your physical limitations has always impressed me. Would you share with us –

JOLENE. I'm so sorry, Mr. Whiteside. We should not draw attention to your physical disability.

LIZ. I wasn't drawing attention… I was asking a question about his process!

JOLENE. We do not discriminate on the basis of physical disability.

LIZ. Are you kidding?

JOLENE. It's unconstitutional. *(to* **EVERETT***)* Do you accept our apology?

EVERETT. Nah, I'm gonna call my lawyer right now and sue your ass. *(beat)* Gotcha!

(fake laughter all around)

TED. I'd like to know the answer to that actually.

JOLENE. You don't have to answer.

EVERETT. I'll answer anything for twenty grand! What's the question again?

TED. How do you create such immense work, considering you're in a wheelchair? The skeleton sculpture's got to be ten feet tall. What's it made of, by the way?

EVERETT. Toilet paper, cardboard, tampons, glue.

TED. Amazing. And how did you piece it all together?

EVERETT. I laid myself down on the floor for that one.

TED. I don't follow.

EVERETT. I laid down on the floor and glued that baby together bit by bit. Didn't stand him up til he was done.

TED. That's impressive.

LIZ. You should see Everett at work. He lies on the floor, assembling one section at a time, then he drags himself across the floor, doing a sort of army crawl, to put the whole thing together.

TED. Incredible. The way you describe it, Liz, it's crystal clear.

EDIE. I don't know how you do it.

EVERETT. Don't have a choice, do I?

JOLENE. Dwayne, did you have a question for Mr. Whiteside?

DWAYNE. Yes. Mr. Whiteside.

EVERETT. Call me Everett.

DWAYNE. Everett. What exactly is your work saying about the Bible?

EVERETT. Whatever you want it to say.

DWAYNE. Right. But as an artist myself, I can tell you: intention is key.

LIZ. Everett shouldn't have to interpret his work for us. That's not the artist's job.

JOLENE. Then what are we all doing here? I thought you wanted to give Everett a voice in the selection process.

LIZ. Yes, but that's different than…

JOLENE. Do you want to give Everett a voice or have I misunderstood something?

LIZ. Forget it.

JOLENE. Mr. Whiteside?

EVERETT. What was the question?

JOLENE. Dwayne?

DWAYNE. What does your work say about the Bible?

EVERETT. That's right. That's right.

DWAYNE. Take the skeleton sculpture, for example. What inspired it?

EVERETT. Ezekiel in the valley of the dry bones.

DWAYNE. Okay… So what I'm wondering…he's a skeleton, right?

EVERETT. Yes.

DWAYNE. So why does he have such a large, you know…?

EVERETT. You wanna know why the sculpture has a big dick?

DWAYNE. Yes. Skeletons don't have those.

EVERETT. You know what the story of Ezekiel's about, Dwayne?

DWAYNE. Not really, no.

EVERETT. It's about resurrection. About God's power to breathe life into death. God looked down on them bones and said, *I will breathe in you and you will come to life! Then you will know that I am God!* Nobody else can make that kind of shit happen. Only God.

DWAYNE. I see. But skeleton don't have…it's an anatomical fact.

EDIE. Oh Dwayne, it's perfectly obvious. The largess of the cock is a symbol of God's omnipotent creative power. *(to **EVERETT**)* I think you could make it even bigger.

EVERETT. Omnipotent creative power. I like that. You should put that in the book, Liz.

JOLENE. What book?

LIZ. Nothing, there's no book.

EVERETT. She didn't tell you? Liz is gonna write a book about me. She already has a cover.

LIZ. I'm just in the research phase.

JOLENE. That sounds like a conflict of interest.

LIZ. I haven't written a book. I'm thinking about it. There's no conflict of interest.

JOLENE. Then why have you been hiding it?

LIZ. I haven't been hiding it; my academic research is none of your business.

JOLENE. It's my business when you lobby the council to spend tax dollars on your research subject.

LIZ. Oh give me a break!

EDIE. Everett, if you were awarded this grant, how would you use the money to further your career as an artist?

EVERETT. How's that?

TED. Perhaps you'd like to take an art class at the university?

EVERETT. Nope.

TED. Purchase supplies for a showing?

EVERETT. Nope.

TED. Any ideas at all?

EVERETT. I'd buy some more space heaters, I can tell you that right now. This barn gets cold in winter, and that Walmart shit don't do the trick.

LIZ. Unlike the other candidate, Everett doesn't have a stable income. The grant would help him meet his fundamental needs. Artists need food and warm shelter, just like the rest of us. There's no shame in that.

DWAYNE. No, there's not, but we want to see that the money goes to good use.

TED. Is there a better purpose than ensuring people are warm, safe and fed?

EDIE. One of the stipulations of the grant is financial need.

LIZ. And originality of vision. Even if we don't see eye to eye on interpreting Everett's work, we can all agree there is nothing else like it.

JOLENE. Mr. Whiteside, have you ever been convicted of a felony?

LIZ. Now that's completely inappropriate!

JOLENE. I'm sorry if I've offended you, Liz, but it's one of our by-laws. We cannot distribute grant money to convicted felons. Right, Dwayne?

DWAYNE. Technically, Jolene is right.

LIZ. Why didn't we ask Rick Duffy if he was a convicted felon?

JOLENE. Rick Duffy is a high school teacher; they vet those. It's a simple question. Mr. Whiteside, have you ever been convicted of a felony.

(pause)

EVERETT. No.

JOLENE. You sound a little uncertain.

EVERETT. They tried to frame me, but I got away!

JOLENE. Who tried to frame you?

LIZ. Everett? Remember what / we talked about. Focus.

EVERETT. They want my house, my bank, my clothes, my shoes –

JOLENE. Who?

EVERETT. They's some greedy muthafuckers.

LIZ. Let's give Everett a couple of minutes to collect himself!

JOLENE. Who is after you?

EVERETT. Uncle Sam.

LIZ. Everett has some back taxes to pay, and he's prone to / exaggerate the situation.

JOLENE. You owe Uncle Sam money?

EVERETT. No! He wants to steal it to pay his superiors.

JOLENE. His superiors?

EVERETT. You seen 'em. You all seen 'em. They got eyes everywhere.

LIZ. I really think it's time for a break!

JOLENE. Who's got eyes?

EVERETT. The Masons. They got Uncle Sam in their pocket.

JOLENE. They do?

LIZ. I could really use some tea, Everett?

EVERETT. And you know whose on top of them? The greedy muthafuckers running the whole shebang?

JOLENE. No, who?

EVERETT. The Jews.

(silence)

JOLENE. Mr. Whiteside, thank you so much for having us to your studio.

EVERETT. That's it? I'm done?

JOLENE. Yes, I would say so. We are definitely finished with you.

Intermission

Scene Six

(Thirty minutes later. **EVERETT**'s *barn.* **LIZ** *has surrendered to the table, her arms over her head.)*

*(***TED** *enters.)*

TED. Hey… I've been waiting… I mean, did I leave my phone? Where's Everett?

LIZ. Loretta took him to the grocery store.

TED. Are you okay?

LIZ. No. Everett has said a lot of crazy shit in front of me. A lot. But nothing as good as that. He's been saving that for a special occasion.

TED. Why'd you ever think he'd interview well?

LIZ. We've been practicing. He's very intelligent actually, just…

TED. Paranoid?

LIZ. Yes. Clinically.

TED. You might've said.

LIZ. You're right. The history of art is made up of the most dysfunctional people on the planet. Everyone knows about Van Gogh, but Jackson Pollock was severely depressed, Munch suffered acute anxiety, Carravaggio shot a man – Everett never did that!

TED. That we know of.

LIZ. I mean, a stint in the asylum is basically an MFA. *(beat)* Who am I kidding? It's over.

TED. Cheer up, it's not the end of the world, is it?

LIZ. Everett owes ten thousand dollars in back taxes. The bank is going to repossess this barn. My book will never get written!

TED. Well, technically we haven't voted yet, and we don't meet till Thursday. Maybe we can keep him in the running.

LIZ. How?

TED. It's obvious he's mentally ill. Explain his condition to the council.

LIZ. Did you see the glee on Jolene's face?

TED. Yeah, but it's not just up to her, is it?

LIZ. Can you imagine Everett spouting off like that to a reporter?

TED. Lucky for us, then.

LIZ. Why?

TED. Who do you think covers the arts for the Ellis County Banner Herald?

LIZ. I have no idea. I don't read the Ellis County Banner Herald.

TED. Nor should you. But trust me, there is nothing Everett could say that I'd find newsworthy.

LIZ. You're the reporter.

TED. Yes. Arts, Sport, and Obituaries. Trust me, you can do this. We can do this. *(pause)* Hang on – I have an idea.

(**TED** *takes out his phone and dials.*)

LIZ. Who are you calling?

(*He holds out his hand to silence her.*)

TED. Hey Dwayne, Ted here. It's about this grant business. *(pause)* You know what I can't stop thinking about? Your Vice Presidents. *(pause)* I do say. They're so… Presidential. And yet not. Precisely! Dwayne, I think you're the real deal. *(pause)* I do. And you know who else thinks so? Liz. Liz thinks you're the real deal too, and she has a PhD –

LIZ. MA –

TED. MA in art history. *(pause)* Cool. Look, since Everett's shot himself in the foot, we, Liz and I, think you should throw your hat back into the ring. What do you say? *(pause)*

Well, let's face it, you're as much a minority as Rick Duffy. Go back to your family tree. I'm willing to bet you're one-sixteenth something too. *(pause)* Twenty thousand buckaroos, Dwayne. *(pause)* That's a good bloke. Byeeee.

(He hangs up.)

There you go. Dwayne will throw his hat back into the ring and won't be able to vote. You and I will vote for Everett, Edie and Jolene will vote for Rick, so all you have to do now is break Edie, which shouldn't be too hard since underneath the polite veneer, she can't stand Jolene.

LIZ. Oh my God. You are a player.

TED. I've been told I have certain gifts…

LIZ. You could've been a Politician.

TED. Yeah…too bad they're all wankers.

(They laugh.)

(pause)

LIZ. You must really hate your wife.

TED. Yes, but that's not why I'm doing it.

LIZ. I know. He's really special, isn't he?

TED. Who?

LIZ. Everett.

TED. Oh no, I think Everett's crap.

LIZ. Then why are you fighting for him?

TED. Not him. You, actually.

LIZ. Me?

TED. You, how did you put it? You unmoor me.

LIZ. Oh.

TED. Is that an "oh no" or "oh goody?"

LIZ. I don't know.

TED. I know, I'm old enough to be your father –

LIZ. No, you're not.

TED. I am.

LIZ. Okay, yeah.

TED. But I can't stop thinking about you. You are, in a word, exquisite. Now that I've gotten that off my chest, you're free to go. Cheers, then. Thanks for your time. *(beat)* You're still here.

LIZ. Yes.

TED. I don't repulse you completely?

LIZ. No. It's just…when you haven't.…when no one has complimented you for a long time, it's hard to know if you're weak in the knees from the mere flattery, or from the actual person behind the flattery.

TED. But you are, in fact, weak in the knees?

LIZ. *(surprising herself)*
Yes.

(They kiss passionately, if somewhat awkwardly, and just as he's backing her onto the table, she stops him.)

TED. What's wrong?

LIZ. This is just casual, right?

TED. Oh yeah, sure, casual.

(They kiss again. This time, **TED** *stops.)*

LIZ. What's wrong?

TED. It's just…can we cover up Ezekiel there? He's staring at us.

LIZ. Why don't you just close your eyes?

(He does.)

(Blackout.)

Scene Seven

(JOLENE*'s working in the gallery.*)

(DWAYNE *enters.*)

DWAYNE. Knock, knock.

JOLENE. Hi Dwayne.

DWAYNE. Do you have a minute? I'd like to speak with you.

JOLENE. I'm expecting a call, Dwayne.

DWAYNE. It won't take long.

JOLENE. Fine. What's going on?

DWAYNE. The fact of the matter is, Cheryl and I have been having some…um…trouble in the bedroom department.

JOLENE. I don't think *(this is appropriate)* –

DWAYNE. Just hear me out. I still find Cheryl plenty attractive, mind you. But after getting laid off and all the stress. Well, we've had some difficulties, if you follow.

JOLENE. I'm following.

DWAYNE. So we've been spicing it up lately. Acting out one another's fantasies. That kind of thing.

JOLENE. I really don't see what this has to do with me –

DWAYNE. I've wanted to try out a three way my whole life.

JOLENE. Ooooo-kay. You don't need to go any further.

DWAYNE. I don't?

JOLENE. Nope.

DWAYNE. But I haven't even *(gotten to the heart of it)* –

JOLENE. Stop right there. Let me say, first, I'm flattered. I'm very, very flattered.

DWAYNE. How come?

JOLENE. That you thought of me.

DWAYNE. For what?

JOLENE. It's okay. We're both adults. But I must say, although Ted and I have our issues – don't we all

– I am committed to remaining in a monogamous marriage, one that doesn't involve third parties. Okay?

DWAYNE. Oh, you thought. Oh. No. That's not –

JOLENE. It's okay.

DWAYNE. No, really, I wasn't going to ask you.

JOLENE. Fine. Let's just pretend it never happened. Good idea.

DWAYNE. No, we already had the three-way.

JOLENE. Without me?

DWAYNE. Yeah. I would never. Trust me, I wouldn't dream of asking you to join Cheryl and me in the bedroom department.

JOLENE. You wouldn't?

DWAYNE. No, ma'am.

JOLENE. Why not?

DWAYNE. Oh. You look great. You're very attractive to *me*. I just don't think you're Cheryl's taste.

JOLENE. Why, what's Cheryl's taste?

DWAYNE. We, I mean, Cheryl, that is, wanted a younger woman to join us. Younger. With bigger and longer and you know.

JOLENE. Yes, everybody knows.

DWAYNE. Sorry for the misunderstanding.

JOLENE. Why don't you just get to your point?

DWAYNE. Well the only way I could get Cheryl to agree to a three way was if I agreed to one going in the opposite direction.

JOLENE. And what direction is that?

DWAYNE. Two guys, one gal.

JOLENE. Right.

DWAYNE. So we tried that out, too. I set some boundaries, mind you, some very clear boundaries, but I have to tell you, when that young man stood up to get dressed, with the wind caressing us through the open window, and his buttocks, as round and smooth as the moon outside, just within reach, something stirred deep inside me. It did. I can't lie.

JOLENE. What are you trying to tell me, exactly?

DWAYNE. I am one-sixteenth gay.

JOLENE. One-sixteenth.

DWAYNE. That is correct. And as a one-sixteenth homosexual male, I would like to be considered for the Living Wage Grant.

JOLENE. You would.

DWAYNE. Yes, ma'am.

(pause)

JOLENE. How do you propose we explain your minority status to our donors? How do we explain it to the community at large?

DWAYNE. Cheryl and I talked about it, and we think it's best if I'm described as a bi-sexual male. We don't need to go into the whole story.

JOLENE. You and Cheryl spoke about this?

DWAYNE. Cheryl is very open-minded.

JOLENE. So I'm learning.

DWAYNE. And we really need the money.

JOLENE. I see.

DWAYNE. So, do what you gotta do, get everybody on the phone, Dwayne Dean is throwing his hat back into the ring.

JOLENE. Dwayne.

DWAYNE. Yeah?

JOLENE. Do you remember the criteria of the Living Wage Grant?

DWAYNE. Sure. The artist has to live in Ellis County for five years. No problem there. He's gotta have financial need. Done. And preferably be a minority, which I've just demonstrated right before your very eyes.

JOLENE. You missed one.

DWAYNE. How's that?

JOLENE. Artistic excellence.

DWAYNE. That's a given, right? *(pause)* Right?

JOLENE. Dwayne, think of excellence as a spectrum. Say, Michelangelo is at one end. The right end, along with Carravagio and Van Gogh. Bob Ross is dead center. Our friend Rick Duffy, left of him. You, as a beginning artist, are far, far, far, far left.

DWAYNE. Wow.

JOLENE. I know it's hard to hear.

DWAYNE. You put me on the same spectrum as Van Gogh.

JOLENE. On the other side of the spectrum.

DWAYNE. That is so encouraging!

JOLENE. Think of it this way. Although you show promise, you are still a beginner.

DWAYNE. That's true.

JOLENE. And like all beginners, you make mistakes. That's part of the artistic process. Discovering what not to do.

DWAYNE. I don't follow.

JOLENE. Take your Vice Presidents.

DWAYNE. Okay.

JOLENE. For a novice, they are excellent. But when you're further down the road, you may find them a touch derivative.

DWAYNE. What do you mean?

JOLENE. Your vice-presidential series lacks originality.

DWAYNE. But they're vice presidents.

JOLENE. Yes.

DWAYNE. Not presidents. If I'd painted Presidents, then you'd have a point. But I specifically chose vice-presidents for their originality.

JOLENE. In style. They lack originality in style.

DWAYNE. I hadn't considered that.

JOLENE. You're not ready to compete with mature artists like Rick Duffy, and even Everett Whiteside, who I have to admit, possesses a very original vision, if nothing else.

DWAYNE. Wow.

JOLENE. I'm sorry.

DWAYNE. This comes as a blow.

JOLENE. Don't let it discourage you. Get back into the studio. Paint late into the night, every night, and in three or four or twenty years, you will develop into the artist…only you can be.

DWAYNE. But I just have so much to share!

JOLENE. So you get to work refining the vehicle of all that sharing.

DWAYNE. What am I going to tell Cheryl?

(beat)

JOLENE. You tell her every artist faces rejection. It's how they handle it that makes them great.

Scene Eight

*(**TED** and **JOLENE**'s bedroom. **TED** is sitting on the bed. He calls **LIZ**.)*

TED. Hey. You're not there. Again. I just want to say the other day was wonderful. Mind blowing, really. I know you're busy – aren't we all – but I've booked a motel for Friday night. The Sunrise Inn. Pink Champagne on ice. See you then. Byeee.

*(**TED** leans back and starts flipping through pictures on his phone.)*

*(**JOLENE** enters in a nightgown.)*

JOLENE. I am in a good mood.

TED. Are you?

JOLENE. Yes. I heard from Bob Duffy today. It's not official, but it looks like our budget will be approved! Of course, he was thrilled to hear Rick is our front-runner for the Living Wage grant.

(She climbs on the bed.)

JOLENE. What are you doing?

TED. Oh, nothing.

*(**TED** quickly puts down his phone.)*

JOLENE. Porn?

TED. No.

JOLENE. Why not? You love porn.

TED. It's not porn. It's Manchester United. They're playing shit, in case you're interested.

JOLENE. I'm not. *(pause)* The bathroom's all yours.

TED. Terrific.

(He stands and takes off his robe, revealing a new pair of tiger stripped bikini briefs.)

JOLENE. That's new.

TED. What? Oh right. They were on sale.

(He steps past her and into the bathroom. Curiosity piqued, she picks up his phone and scrolls through the pictures.)

JOLENE. Ted?

TED. *(off)*
   Yeah?

JOLENE. This isn't porn.

   (TED returns to the bedroom.)

TED. What's that?

JOLENE. This isn't porn, and it isn't Manchester United either. Why are you looking at pictures of Liz and Everett Whiteside?

   (pause)

TED. I was just taking another look at his work, if you must know.

JOLENE. Why?

TED. Because…frankly, I think he might be the real deal.

JOLENE. The real deal.

TED. That's right.

JOLENE. *(amused)*
   How do you know?

TED. What?

JOLENE. That Everett's the *real deal?*

TED. It's difficult to explain really. It's not rational. It's more of a spiritual thing.

JOLENE. Spiritual?

TED. That's right.

JOLENE. I didn't know you were religious, Ted.

TED. Not religious, no. Spiritual in a more cultural sense.

JOLENE. And what culture is that?

TED. English. You know, in England school children are exposed to culture much earlier than here in the States. When I was just a kid, they herded us onto the bus and into the National Gallery. It made a big impression. Columns. Turrets. Big staircase.

JOLENE. And the art?

TED. Walls covered in paintings by...the masters.

JOLENE. What masters?

TED. All of them.

JOLENE. Can you name a single painting hanging in the National Gallery?

TED. They had lots of...that fellow who did watercolors... lots of ships at sea and all that.

JOLENE. Joseph Turner.

TED. Yes, Joseph Turner! I can't tell you what it meant to me, as a young Englishman to see my play fantasies acted out on the wall in paint. Ships! Cannons! Waves! Arghhh!

JOLENE. Fascinating. And all this time, I thought your childhood fantasies involved playing drums for The Who.

TED. That too.

JOLENE. But secretly you were an art aficionado!

TED. Not an aficionado, no. I wouldn't say that. I'm only saying, when I was in school, we visited the greatest museums in the world. Of course we did, they were only a couple of hours away. But you, you didn't have the same privileges growing up here, how could you – miles from civilization.

JOLENE. No, we were lucky to have electricity!

TED. Now, it's true that some of you have risen above it, but cultural appreciation is a learned skill in America. In England, we're born to it.

JOLENE. Ted.

TED. What?

JOLENE. You're American.

TED. By marriage.

JOLENE. When I met you at that Dead show, you couldn't throw away your passport fast enough!

TED. Citizenship is a lot like marriage. After the initial rush, the romance wears thin.

(*pause*)

(**JOLENE** *picks up the phone and clicks though the pictures.*)

JOLENE. You know, Ted, maybe you're right. Perhaps as an Englishman, you have access to a deep cultural consciousness I hadn't considered before. Why don't you turn your finely tuned lens to this sculpture here.

TED. I never said finely tuned...

JOLENE. I'd love to hear what an *Englishman* has to say about this paper maiche head on a platter.

TED. What – right now?

JOLENE. Yes. This head here. The one Liz is holding up in the picture.

TED. Well...for starters...it's made of found materials. Milk cartons. Toilet rolls. I believe there's a bit of cereal box around the nose.

JOLENE. And that's significant why?

TED. It demonstrates great moral imagination!

JOLENE. *Moral* imagination? How is that different from your garden variety sort?

TED. It has more fiber. Like a good cereal. Which ties into the cereal box.

JOLENE. Go on.

TED. The subject is a fellow from the Bible, whatshisname...

JOLENE. John the Baptist?

TED. Yes! And as such, he has great theological import.

JOLENE. What theological issues does the sculpture explore? Specifically.

TED. It's about...losing one's head. Both literally and metaphorically speaking. The fellow has lost his head for Jesus! And this means...he is walking around headless. As one does. In heaven. Where all things are possible.

JOLENE. You are full of complete shit, you know that?

TED. So I don't have the vocabulary for art criticism. All I can say is: I look at this photograph, and I'm moved.

JOLENE. By what?

TED. By her beauty.

JOLENE. Her?

TED. Its. I mean, its.

JOLENE. Oh my God.

TED. Or him. It's a him, I think.

JOLENE. You have a crush on Liz.

TED. It's not what you think.

(*JOLENE starts to laugh.*)

JOLENE. Well that explains everything!

TED. What?

JOLENE. This sudden interest in the council and Everett Whiteside. Jockeying for his consideration. You have a crush on Liz.

TED. I do not.

JOLENE. Admit it. You've always had a thing for Asian women.

TED. I have not.

JOLENE. Oh please – do you really want me to pull up your browser history?

TED. That is none of your business.

JOLENE. Ted, I'm not mad. Really. I think it's funny.

TED. Why? You're supposed to be my wife!

JOLENE. Relax. It's just a crush. I know that. It's not like you're having an affair.

TED. How do you know?

JOLENE. You and Liz. Come on, Ted.

TED. What?

JOLENE. Be realistic.

TED. Is it so unrealistic that another woman might dig me?

JOLENE. No, of course not. I am sure there are plenty of women around town who "dig you", but probably more in your age range.

TED. For your information, Liz finds me plenty attractive!

JOLENE. I'm sure she does, honey.

TED. Attractive enough to have sex with!

JOLENE. Ted.

TED. What?

JOLENE. We all have crushes. It's okay, but you can't let your crush interfere with my job. Our budget is on the line, remember?

TED. That's it? That's all you have to say?

JOLENE. What do you want me to say?

TED. I want you to tell me to STOP SLEEPING WITH THAT WHORE!

(silence)

JOLENE. Ted, I know we have problems.

TED. Yes. Namely, I'm having sexual intercourse with Liz.

JOLENE. Seriously, once our budget has been approved, I'd love to take a trip to Lake Wilson. Budget a little time to re-kindle the flames.

TED. You would?

JOLENE. Yes, it is on my to-do list.

TED. That's it. I'm voting for Everett.

JOLENE. Excuse me?

TED. At Thursday's meeting, I'm voting for Everett and so is Liz.

JOLENE. Don't you dare.

TED. That got your attention, didn't it?

*(**TED** exits.)*

Scene Nine

(EVERETT's barn. He sits behind his table, working, perhaps sorting trash or stripping cans.)

(A plate of rice crispy treats sits on the table as well.)

(LIZ enters with a box of doughnuts.

LIZ. Hi Everett! *(pause)* Everett?

EVERETT. He ain't here.

LIZ. Where did he go?

EVERETT. You think that muthafucker tells me anything?

LIZ. Okay…can I leave a message for him?

EVERETT. Do I look like the mailman? Am I wearing red, white and blue?

LIZ. Will you at least tell him Liz is looking for him?

EVERETT. No.

LIZ. Why not?

EVERETT. Cause he ain't talking to you.

LIZ. How come?

EVERETT. Cause you made me get all dressed up just to entertain a pack of Indian givers!

LIZ. Well, maybe you'll forgive me when you find out those Indian givers are still considering you for the living wage grant.

EVERETT. You expect me to trust them?

LIZ. I was hoping you might trust me. Friends?

EVERETT. Do friends help friends?

LIZ. Absolutely.

EVERETT. Alright then.

LIZ. Good. Because I have this idea for my book, and I wanted to take another look at John the Baptist. Where is he?

EVERETT. Hey Liz.

LIZ. Yeah?

EVERETT. You got some money I can borrow?

LIZ. What, me personally?

EVERETT. Yeah.

LIZ. I don't think that's appropriate.

EVERETT. Why not? We're friends, right?

LIZ. Yes, but...

EVERETT. Well your friend needs money, Liz.

LIZ. I know.

> (**EVERETT** *takes a letter out of his pocket and hands it to* **LIZ.** *She reads it.*)

What's this?

EVERETT. They're turning the screws, but I ain't going nowhere. No siree! They can bring all the bulldozers they want, but I ain't leaving.

LIZ. You know what? This is a first notice. They're not going to auction off the Barn tomorrow. There's still time –

EVERETT. I ain't asking for the whole pot, Liz. Just something to hold 'em over. Loretta said I could pay 'em off in installments, like layaway.

LIZ. I would loan you something, Everett, but I don't actually make much money.

EVERETT. You look like you got money to me. You got a nice car.

LIZ. My Taurus? I bought it used. I still make payments.

EVERETT. So? That's a nice car, and you got them shiny, leather shoes on.

LIZ. I got these at Payless.

EVERETT. And you got one of them robot phones.

LIZ. I need it for work.

EVERETT. Liz.

LIZ. What?

EVERETT. You got money.

LIZ. I have some money, yes. Enough to take care of myself and save a little for retirement. I don't have money for extras.

EVERETT. That robot phone is extra.

LIZ. My students email me –

EVERETT. I'm not talking about the whole pot. How about two grand?

LIZ. Everett, this conversation is making me uncomfortable.

EVERETT. Well, this whole god-damn world makes me uncomfortable!

LIZ. I know. I'm sorry.

EVERETT. I tell you what. From now on, if you want to see my work, I'm charging you admission.

LIZ. That's not fair.

EVERETT. Why not? You using me. I might as well get paid.

LIZ. I'm not using you. I'm writing a book about you.

EVERETT. Oh yeah?

LIZ. Yes.

EVERETT. Then where's the book at? You hiding it somewhere?

LIZ. I'm not done with it.

EVERETT. You ain't even started it.

LIZ. I'm in the research phase.

EVERETT. It's so far up your ass, you can't even see it. Hello book, it's Liz, are you up there?

LIZ. You know, Everett, for some of us, churning out work isn't so easy. It takes time, but I am going to write this book, and I'm doing it for you.

EVERETT. Oh that's right. You a right bright saint. Doing everything you can for little old me. Thank you ma'am, you sure is good to me.

LIZ. Now that is really unfair.

EVERETT. I'm not an idiot. You're writing that book for you, to see your own name in print, get you that big promotion on the hill.

LIZ. Then you don't know anything, Everett, because the last thing I want is a promotion in this po-dunk town on that hill of beans college. I am writing this book to get out!

EVERETT. Just so we're straight!

LIZ. Oh, we're straight.

EVERETT. That'll be two thousand dollars, then. You can leave the money by the rice crispy treats.

LIZ. The rice crispy treats your girlfriend left you?

EVERETT. Loretta ain't my girlfriend.

LIZ. No, she's not. She's your social worker, and you know what she told me? If you had just followed the budget she made for you, you wouldn't be in this mess in the first place.

EVERETT. No, no, no! That bitch wants me to go on food stamps!

LIZ. Oh, you're too proud for food stamps but not to ask for two thousand dollars?

EVERETT. You think I'm gonna take food from Uncle Sam, when he's been living in my asshole? I THOUGHT YOU WERE ON MY SIDE!

LIZ. I am. I'm sorry. I am on your side.

EVERETT. Then when you gonna start acting like it?

(**LIZ** *pulls out her wallet. She hands* **EVERETT** *all the money inside.*)

LIZ. Sixty-three dollars and thirty-two cents.

EVERETT. That's not enough.

LIZ. It's all I have.

EVERETT. When the bulldozers come, I ain't going nowhere.

LIZ. I'm going to get you that money. You have my word.

Scene Ten

(JOLENE and LIZ face off in EDIE's living room.)

JOLENE. Fancy meeting you here.

LIZ. I just stopped by to pay Edie a visit.

JOLENE. How kind of you. How considerate.

(EDIE enters with her tea trolley.)

EDIE. I wasn't expecting company but since you're here.

(She pours from a bottle of cooking sherry into the teacups.)

LIZ. Edie, I came by to talk about Everett. I'm just mortified by how his interview went.

JOLENE. We absolutely cannot consider him. He's an anti-Semite.

LIZ. No, no he's not. That's why I came by –

JOLENE. And he's an anti-Masonite.

EDIE. Oh, who cares about them? *(waving the sherry)* More tea?

JOLENE.	LIZ.
No.	The truth is: he's mentally ill.

JOLENE. That's not an excuse.

LIZ. Everett is clinically paranoid. He's not an anti-Semite!

EDIE. Liz.

LIZ. What?

EDIE. Don't tell Jolene, but I agree with you completely.

JOLENE. Were we at the same interview?

EDIE. It's clear Everett's brain has been addled. Perhaps he was shaken as a baby. Or fell from a tree. Oh! That would explain the wheelchair!

LIZ. Actually, he's been diagnosed by a licensed psychiatrist –

JOLENE. This is not up for debate. I refuse to consider a candidate who would alienate our Jewish constituency!

LIZ. Do we have a Jewish constituency?

EDIE. Yes.

JOLENE. Do we?

EDIE. My maiden name was Goldberg.

JOLENE. Really?

EDIE. Yes, I was born a Goldberg from a very short line of Kansan Jews.

LIZ. Well, Edie, I'm just thankful you can see the true man behind the illness.

EDIE. That doesn't mean I'm voting for him.

(**EDIE** *reaches for the bottle and tries to pour; it's empty.*)

Excuse me, this pot needs refilling.

(She exits.)

JOLENE. You are putting the entire arts council at risk.

LIZ. How? By advocating for a deserving minority artist? Look me in the eye and tell me you don't think Everett has something special. Even you know the difference between a Monet and a Kinkade.

JOLENE. Do you know what we fund besides this one grant?

LIZ. I'm aware –

JOLENE. Two elementary school art teachers, three summer camps, art awareness week, photography contests, / drawing classes at the library.

LIZ. I've read the annual report.

JOLENE. Is Everett Whiteside really worth jeopardizing all that?

(**EDIE** *returns with a bottle of creme de menthe.*)

EDIE. It's all I could find. Vernon was the worst kind of teetotaler. You'd think a man who could shoot a coyote between the eyes could stomach a little hooch now and then, but no, Vernon drank like a Mormon.

LIZ. Edie, remember how impressed you were by / Everett's work –

EDIE. My parents begged me not to marry him, you know.

JOLENE. No, I didn't.

EDIE. I married him just to spite Mother. She wouldn't let me wear pants. It was 1963. All the girls wore pants. But no, she said, that's not our way. We were Mennonites.

LIZ. I thought you were Jewish.

EDIE. We were converts. Mennonite Jews. I didn't even know what sex was until I married Vernon. Imagine my surprise!

(*JOLENE tries to steer EDIE back to the couch.*)

JOLENE. Okay, time to park this train back in the station.

EDIE. Exactly!

LIZ. I'm sorry, Edie, I don't understand.

EDIE. The man parks his train in your station.

LIZ. No, I mean, why won't you vote for Everett?

EDIE. I've been packing up Vernon's things.

LIZ.	**JOLENE.**
Okay…	Good for you.

EDIE. And you know what I found in his underwear drawer? Photographs!

LIZ. Porn?

EDIE. No. The photographs were of us. Our honeymoon backpacking on the Natchez Trail.

JOLENE. How romantic.

EDIE. The birth of Vernon Jr., at home without anesthetics. Our silver anniversary dinner in a yurt. And in every single picture, I look so…

JOLENE. Young? Radiant?

EDIE. Unhappy. I think I had a miserable marriage and didn't even know it.

JOLENE. So were you really miserable? If a tree falls in the woods and no one sees it, is it really felled?

EDIE. Ask the tree! I spent my whole marriage doing whatever he wanted. I wanted to give birth in a hospital as God intended, but no, Vernon insisted I take hold of the reigns of my womanhood and give birth like a man!

JOLENE. He could be overenthusiastic.

EDIE. He was a narcissist. And you know who the narcissist would have voted for?

JOLENE. Yes.

LIZ. No, who?

EDIE. Everett.

LIZ. Really? Doesn't Rick seem more to his taste?

EDIE. Vernon couldn't stand Bob Duffy.

JOLENE. Loathed him. There's no way he would have voted for his son.

EDIE. But I can. Take that old man!

LIZ. Let me get this straight. You're going to vote for Rick Duffy to spite your dead husband, because he would have voted for Everett to spite Bob Duffy, Rick's Dad?

EDIE. Yes.

JOLENE. That's right.

LIZ. That's crazy! Maybe it's time to forget what that male chauvinist pig would do. Good riddance to the jerk!

EDIE. How dare you speak about my husband that way!

JOLENE. Have some respect.

LIZ. Look. Every time I see something Everett has created, it makes me see the world anew. Can you honestly say that about Rick Duffy?

JOLENE. *(unconvincingly)*
   Yes.

LIZ. Oh please, Rick Duffy is a complete hack!

JOLENE. Beauty is in the eye of the beholder.

EDIE. That's right. One man's trash is another man's rash.

LIZ. No, I don't accept that. People, as a rule, don't know shit about good art, especially in Kansas.

JOLENE. You live in Kansas.

LIZ. I am from St. Louis!

JOLENE. Well, if I'd known you were from such a cultural mecca –

LIZ. I have an MA in art history. I've published an article in Contemporary Art today –

EDIE. Is anyone else hungry?

(EDIE exits.)

LIZ. An article that was cited in two different dissertations!

JOLENE. If you're such an expert, Liz, why are you teaching at the local community college?

LIZ. It's a tough academic market.

JOLENE. Why aren't you in the Ivy League?

(EDIE returns with a box of cereal. She plops down on the couch and eats from the box, slugging it down with the crème de menthe.)

LIZ. I came where I was needed.

JOLENE. They wouldn't have you, would they?

LIZ. It's true, I have some hiccups with my research.

JOLENE. Couldn't quite cut it. Never as smart as the other Asians.

LIZ. I self-sabotage if you must know. I over think things. Frankly, I am a victim of my own intelligence!

JOLENE. Do you hear yourself?

LIZ. Well at least I don't have to prove my worth by strutting around a little po-dunk arts council like I'm Mussolini!

JOLENE. I don't know what you're talking about. I'm completely fulfilled in my job.

LIZ. Does that make up for your black hole of a marriage?

EDIE. Now that is an excellent question!

JOLENE. Oh, who asked you?

EDIE. I've always wondered, were you knocked up when you got married or just high?

JOLENE. Nobody is interested in your opinions, Edie.

EDIE. That's right. All I'm good for is my dead husband's money.

JOLENE. Well, did you really think you were on the council for your good taste? I mean, look at this couch!

(Beat. EDIE pours the cereal over JOLENE's head.)

EDIE. Now then, you'll have to excuse me while I vomit. You can let yourselves out.

JOLENE. Edie –

EDIE. I'll see you at the meeting tomorrow, when I vote for Everett, as he's more in line with my very bad taste.

(beat)

LIZ. I'm sorry. It's not personal.

EDIE. No. It's just art.

Scene Eleven

(The gallery.)

(LIZ enters first. She finds a seat and arranges herself.)

(TED enters.)

TED. Oh good. I was hoping to catch you alone.

LIZ. Hi Ted.

TED. Did you get my message, about the motel and the you know –

LIZ. Yes…can we talk after the meeting? Alone?

TED. Dirty girl.

LIZ. Talk is not code for sex.

TED. I was just joking. Yes, let's talk. Have a pow wow about our feelings. A real heart to heart. I just haven't felt this good in so long –

LIZ. Afterwards.

TED. Right-o. Cool.

(EDIE enters, wearing sunglasses.)

LIZ. Hi Edie.

EDIE. Hello.

TED. Nothing going on here. We were just talking about David Moyes. What went wrong there? What do you think, Edie?

EDIE. Not so loud.

TED. Oh, had one too many, have you?

(JOLENE enters.)

JOLENE. Good morning, everyone.

(DWAYNE enters, carrying a covered canvas, his clothes splattered with paint.)

DWAYNE. Am I late?

JOLENE. No.

DWAYNE. Good. Before we get to the vote, I have something I'd like to say.

JOLENE. This is not a good time. Can I have everyone's attention please?

DWAYNE. I have something very important to say –

JOLENE. Not now, Dwayne. I've prepared some remarks to get this Council back on track –

DWAYNE. I WILL NOT BE SILENCED!

(silence)

Recently, it came to my attention that my work, while revolutionary in content was lacking in style. So I locked myself in the garage and searched my soul, until like a chick breaking through the shell of his confinement, I was born again. Fasten your seatbelts, folks, and meet Aaron Burr for the first time.

(**DWAYNE** *reveals his painting to the group, unseen by the audience.*)

(pause)

TED. That's very original.

LIZ. I've never seen anything like it.

EDIE. Is that a buttock?

DWAYNE. Yes!

TED. And that?

DWAYNE. Yes!

EDIE. What about that?

DWAYNE. That's the moon. They reflect one another, but they are not the same.

EDIE. Why is the moon wearing a wig?

DWAYNE. Because he's in disguise.

EDIE. As a buttock?

DWAYNE. It's not supposed to be…what's the word…

LIZ. Literal?

DWAYNE. Thank you. It's not literal. It's expressionistic.

JOLENE. Well whatever it is, cover it back up.

DWAYNE. So does that seal the deal? Am I a shoo-in or what?

EDIE. For what, dear?

DWAYNE. The living wage grant!

EDIE. Oh no.

DWAYNE. But the painting –

EDIE. Is terrible. You are a terrible artist, Dwayne, and it's high time you knew it.

DWAYNE. That's funny. You're a hoot, Edie.

JOLENE. It's not a joke, Dwayne.

DWAYNE. So what you're saying is: my work is divisive.

EDIE. We're not divided.

DWAYNE. Tell them, Ted. Liz.

TED. Yeah, he's right. I think Dwayne's great.

DWAYNE. Thank you!

LIZ. Just super.

DWAYNE. They think I'm the real deal.

LIZ. Yep.

TED. Totally.

JOLENE. Ted told you that?

DWAYNE. Yes. He told me to throw my hat back into the ring. Liz too.

JOLENE. Ted and Liz. Liz and Ted.

TED. That's right. I told you: Liz and I are having an affair.

LIZ. You told her? Why would you do that?

DWAYNE. *(to* **EDIE***)*
    You really don't think it's any good?

EDIE. No, Dwayne.*

DWAYNE. Huh.

JOLENE. *(to* **LIZ***)*
    *Wait a minute: you had actual sex with my husband?

TED. Twice!

LIZ. Why would you tell your wife?

TED. I know it's new, but I think what we have together is very special.

(During the following argument, EDIE tends to her hangover, bringing one item after another out of her purse: a fan, a flask, aspirin, etc...)

JOLENE. What?

LIZ. Only if you call a moment of weakness special.*

JOLENE. I have to give it to you Ted.

TED. *A moment of weakness?

JOLENE. I didn't think you had it in you.

LIZ. Yes. I told you it was casual.

JOLENE. Ted –

TED. I know but it evolved into something stronger.

JOLENE. Ted, I'm talking to you!

LIZ. When?

TED. The second time round!

LIZ. No, Ted. I'm sorry.

(pause)

TED. Dwayne, I take it back. You're total shit.

LIZ. Ted, no.

DWAYNE. What?

TED. Yeah, it's all been a ploy, one big fat manipulation / of the female variety.

DWAYNE. What are you saying exactly?

TED. You're crap, man. Total crap. And I'm voting for Rick Duffy!

LIZ. I knew your testicles would dry up the minute I dumped you.

DWAYNE. Does anyone in this room believe in me at all?

JOLENE. Dwayne, can you stop thinking about yourself for one second. I just found out my husband is having an affair.

TED. *(to LIZ)*
You're worse than she is, you know that?

LIZ. I wasn't manipulating you. It just didn't have the same meaning for me / that it had for you.

TED. Did it have any meaning at all?

DWAYNE. I know I'm untrained, but I could go back to school. / With the grant, I could do that.

LIZ. Define meaning.

JOLENE. Dwayne, hell will freeze over before you get one finger on that grant!

DWAYNE. Fine, I'm voting for Everett.

LIZ. Thank you!

DWAYNE. I'm not doing it for you. I'm doing it to spite Jolene.

LIZ. I'll take it. Ted, please don't vote for Rick just to spite me.

TED. I'm sorry, but if Dwayne is voting to spite Jolene. I can certainly vote to spite you.

JOLENE. What? Don't you want to spite me?

TED. I fucked her to spite you, isn't that enough?

DWAYNE. No, everything has to be about Jolene.

JOLENE. Oh, grow a pair, Dwayne.

DWAYNE. I'm having suicidal thoughts. If you have them, you're supposed to say something. / I'm having suicidal thoughts.

JOLENE. Were you ever going to tell me?

TED. I did tell you. You didn't believe me!

(**EVERETT** *wheels himself into the room.*)

EVERETT. I'm here!

LIZ. Everett, this is not a good time –

EVERETT. You told Loretta to bring me.

LIZ. AFTER the meeting! We haven't even voted yet!

DWAYNE. You know who I feel like right now? Van Gogh.

JOLENE. Don't you dare compare yourself to Van Gogh. (*to* **EVERETT**) Mr. Whiteside, I'm going to have to insist that you wait outside.

EVERETT. *(to* **LIZ**)
You said it was in the bag!

LIZ. There've been some complications.

EVERETT. Uncle Sam got to you, didn't he?

DWAYNE. Nobody appreciated Van Gogh in his lifetime.

LIZ. You have nothing in common with Van Gogh; trust me, I have an MA. / *(to TED)* I feel so betrayed by you right now.*

JOLENE. Oh, we know!

EVERETT. Uncle Sam is with us now.

TED. *Betrayed? You publically humiliated me.

JOLENE. Hello? If anyone should feel betrayed right now, it's me!

TED. *(to JOLENE)*
   Oh now you have feelings –

JOLENE. Of course I have feelings!

TED. Just not for me.*

EVERETT. *(to LIZ)*
   You fooled me before but not again.

LIZ. Everett, please, will you wait outside while I fix this!

EVERETT. I ain't waiting outside for you like some chauffeur.

JOLENE. *What are you talking about?

TED. I am your last priority. A dot on your to-do list.

JOLENE. No, that's not true.

DWAYNE. My God, I'm exactly like Van Gogh!

LIZ. You are nothing like Van Gogh, Dwayne.

DWAYNE. Then why do I have an irresistible urge to cut off my ear?

JOLENE. Because that's the only way you'll / ever have anything in common with Van Gogh!

EVERETT. I am onto you!

LIZ.	**JOLENE.**
Everett, please, you are just making things worse!	Ted, I have built my life around you.

DWAYNE. Vincent, can you hear me?

EVERETT.
    You been playin' me this whole time.

LIZ.
    No, that's not true.

EVERETT.
    You promised to get Uncle Sam off my back.

LIZ.
    That's not what I said.

TED. More like humiliated.

DWAYNE. Vincent, can you see me?

EVERETT.
Acting like you an angel. You ain't no angel.

LIZ.
    I can't solve all your problems –

EVERETT.
    Acting like a savior. You sure as hell ain't that.

LIZ. I cannot be responsible for you!

TED. Name one thing you like about me.

EVERETT. I know who you are. I see through that mask.

TED. HA!

JOLENE. Fine, I don't like you.

LIZ.
    What am I, Everett?

JOLENE. But I love you!

EVERETT. You know!

TED.
    Yeah, around my shortcomings!

JOLENE.
    Well, somebody has to support us.

TED.
    How do you think that makes me feel?

JOLENE.
    I don't know, Ted, how about supported?

JOLENE.
    How can you say that?

TED.
    Because they only thing I know how to do is let you down.

JOLENE.
    No, that's not true.

TED.
    Thank you!

JOLENE. Isn't that enough?

TED.   **LIZ.**

   No!   A Mason? A Jew?

(**DWAYNE** *pulls out a pocket knife.*)

DWAYNE. I have a knife!

(Everyone ignore **DWAYNE**.*)*

EVERETT. You're the anti-Christ!

TED. I'm leaving you!

JOLENE. Oh good luck!

DWAYNE. I'm warning you!

JOLENE. Oh for fuck's sake, Dwayne. JUST DO IT!

(**DWAYNE** *cuts off the top of his ear and throws it to the ground.*)

(beat)

EVERETT. That is one crazy muthafucker.

DWAYNE. Holy Mother of God that hurts!

(**EDIE** *takes center stage.*)

EDIE. Jolene, get two bags of ice from the freezer. Liz, stop the bleeding. Ted, call 911. Dwayne, sit.

(Everybody obeys **EDIE**.*)*

(**JOLENE** *returns with the ice.*)

EDIE. *(to* **JOLENE***)*

Put one bag on the wound. Give the other one to me.

(**EDIE** *takes off her scarf and uses it to pick up the ear. She puts it in the bag.*)

TED. The ambulance will be here in five.

EDIE. Thank you. That gives us plenty of time. NOW EVERYONE SIT. Vernon and I did not match the living wage grant so you all might act out your personal grievances. Now while we sit here and wait for the ambulance, we are going to vote for the artist we each think is most deserving, and then I'm resigning and never giving the Arts Council another cent. Have I made myself clear?

TED. Yeah.

LIZ. Fine.

JOLENE. Whatever!

(**DWAYNE** *whimpers.*)

EDIE. Good. Now everyone close your eyes. *(Pause)* All in favor of giving the living wage grant to Rick Duffy, raise your hand.

(**DWAYNE** *raises his hand.*)

(**TED** *raises his hand.*)

(**EDIE** *raises her hand.*)

I'm sorry, Everett. Rick Duffy it is.

(**JOLENE** *and* **LIZ** *take in the vote, then stare at one another. The others lower their hands.*)

LIZ. You. All this time.

JOLENE. What can I say? Everett is a visionary. Rick Duffy is a hack.

(sirens)

EDIE. Now let's get Dwayne outside.

(**EDIE** *helps* **DWAYNE** *up and out.*)

(**TED** *and* **JOLENE** *follow.*)

(**LIZ** *turns to* **EVERETT**.)

LIZ. I'm sorry.

EVERETT. You can take my house, my coat, my shoes. I ain't goin' nowhere.

(**LIZ** *exits.*)

(**EVERETT** *sits there for a beat.*)

(Then he wheels over to the trash can and starts pulling out items one by one and placing them on the table:)

(A soda can)

(A coffee cup)

(A crumpled piece of paper)

(A cracked light bulb)

(He holds the light bulb up to the light, examining it from every direction.)

(The gallery transforms into **EVERETT***'s studio, and he gets back to work.)*

End of Play

www.ingramcontent.com/pod-product-compliance
Lightning Source LLC
Chambersburg PA
CBHW071840290426
44109CB00017B/1886